Cruising Memories A BOATER'S DIARY

Mystic Seaport Museum Stores, Inc.
Mystic, Connecticut 06355

Foreword

This practical record-keeping diary is designed for the yachtsman and his crew to aid in their enjoyment of the water. Created by yachtsmen for yachtsmen, the Boater's Diary offers opportunities of adventure and rewarding memory joggers that can be kept and treasured for generations to come. All boaters, from those who enjoy small craft to those who enjoy extended luxury cruises, will find hours of relaxation and extended welcomed use of this book.

This Boater's Diary is the first book of its kind to offer boaters a journal in which to record interesting and fun facts about cruises. This book can be stored next to the Ship's Log but used to record the non-technical aspects of your cruise; the bits of information, often neglected, that make boating and remembering boating fun.

Ample pages are here for you to create a keepsake of cruising memories that will be cherished for many years to come.

Happy boating!

Cruising Memories of the Yacht:

_____

This journal is being kept by:

_____

Yacht Particulars

NAME OF YACHT: _____

OWNER: _____

TYPE OF YACHT: _____

HAILING PORT: _____

DESIGNER: _____

BUILDER: _____

YEAR BUILT: _____ YEAR PURCHASED: _____

REGISTRATION NUMBER: _____

LENGTH: _____ BEAM: _____ DRAFT: _____

VERTICAL CLEARANCE: _____ TONNAGE: *Net* _____ *Gross* _____

SAILS: _____

ENGINE MAKE: _____ *Model* _____ *Year* _____

TANKAGE: *Fuel* _____ *Water* _____ *Other* _____

AUXILLIARY EQUIPMENT: _____

HULL COLOR: _____

RADIO CALL SIGN: _____

_____

INSURANCE: *Broker* _____

          Address _____ *Phone* _____

_____

          Policy # _____ *Firm* _____

OTHER _____

_____

_____

_____

_____

_____

_____

_____

_____

_____

_____

OTHER FACTS ABOUT OUR YACHT: _____

Friends
We Met Along the Way

NAME: _____

ADDRESS: _____

CITY, STATE, ZIP: _____

PHONE: _____

_____

NAME: _____

ADDRESS: _____

CITY, STATE, ZIP: _____

PHONE: _____

_____

NAME: _____

ADDRESS: _____

CITY, STATE, ZIP: _____

PHONE: _____

_____

NAME: _____

ADDRESS: _____

CITY, STATE, ZIP: _____

PHONE: _____

_____

NAME: _____

ADDRESS: _____

CITY, STATE, ZIP: _____

PHONE: _____

_____

NAME: _____

ADDRESS: _____

CITY, STATE, ZIP: _____

PHONE: _____

_____

NAME: _____

ADDRESS: _____

CITY, STATE, ZIP: _____

PHONE: _____

_____

NAME: _____

ADDRESS: _____

CITY, STATE, ZIP: _____

PHONE: _____

_____

NAME: _____

ADDRESS: _____

CITY, STATE, ZIP: _____

PHONE: _____

_____

NAME: _____

ADDRESS: _____

CITY, STATE, ZIP: _____

PHONE: _____

_____

NAME: _____

ADDRESS: _____

CITY, STATE, ZIP: _____

PHONE: _____

_____

NAME: _____

ADDRESS: _____

CITY, STATE, ZIP: _____

PHONE: _____

_____

NAME: _____

ADDRESS: _____

CITY, STATE, ZIP: _____

PHONE: _____

_____

Cruises

Today's Cruise

DAY, DATE: _____

PLANNED DESTINATION: _____

PORT DEPARTED: _____ TIME: _____

PORT ARRIVED: _____ TIME: _____

SKIPPER: _____ CREW: _____

_____

GUESTS ABOARD: _____

_____

WEATHER: _____

WHAT & WHERE WE ATE: _____

_____

_____

_____

_____

WHERE WE SHOPPED & WHAT WE BOUGHT: _____

_____

_____

_____

WHO WE MET: _____

_____

_____

_____

Memorable Things About Today's Cruise

_____

_____

_____

_____

_____

_____

_____

_____

_____

REMINDER FOR NEXT PORT: _____

Today's Cruise

DAY, DATE: _____

PLANNED DESTINATION: _____

PORT DEPARTED: _____ TIME: _____

PORT ARRIVED: _____ TIME: _____

SKIPPER: _____ CREW: _____

_____

GUESTS ABOARD: _____

_____

WEATHER: _____

WHAT & WHERE WE ATE: _____

_____

_____

_____

_____

WHERE WE SHOPPED & WHAT WE BOUGHT: _____

_____

_____

_____

WHO WE MET: _____

_____

_____

_____

Memorable Things About Today's Cruise

_____

_____

_____

_____

_____

_____

_____

_____

_____

REMINDER FOR NEXT PORT: _____

Today's Cruise

DAY, DATE: _____

PLANNED DESTINATION: _____

PORT DEPARTED: _____ TIME: _____

PORT ARRIVED: _____ TIME: _____

SKIPPER: _____ CREW: _____

_____

GUESTS ABOARD: _____

_____

WEATHER: _____

WHAT & WHERE WE ATE: _____

_____

_____

_____

_____

WHERE WE SHOPPED & WHAT WE BOUGHT: _____

_____

_____

_____

WHO WE MET: _____

_____

_____

_____

Memorable Things About Today's Cruise

_____

_____

_____

_____

_____

_____

_____

_____

REMINDER FOR NEXT PORT: _____

Today's Cruise

DAY, DATE: _____

PLANNED DESTINATION: _____

PORT DEPARTED: _____ TIME: _____

PORT ARRIVED: _____ TIME: _____

SKIPPER: _____ CREW: _____

_____

GUESTS ABOARD: _____

_____

WEATHER: _____

WHAT & WHERE WE ATE: _____

_____

_____

_____

_____

WHERE WE SHOPPED & WHAT WE BOUGHT: _____

_____

_____

_____

_____

WHO WE MET: _____

_____

_____

_____

_____

Memorable Things About Today's Cruise

_____

_____

_____

_____

_____

_____

_____

_____

_____

REMINDER FOR NEXT PORT: _____

Today's Cruise

DAY, DATE: _____

PLANNED DESTINATION: _____

PORT DEPARTED: _____ TIME: _____

PORT ARRIVED: _____ TIME: _____

SKIPPER: _____ CREW: _____

_____

GUESTS ABOARD: _____

_____

WEATHER: _____

WHAT & WHERE WE ATE: _____

_____

_____

_____

_____

WHERE WE SHOPPED & WHAT WE BOUGHT: _____

_____

_____

_____

_____

WHO WE MET: _____

_____

_____

_____

_____

Memorable Things About Today's Cruise

_____

_____

_____

_____

_____

_____

_____

_____

_____

REMINDER FOR NEXT PORT: _____

Today's Cruise

DAY, DATE: _____

PLANNED DESTINATION: _____

PORT DEPARTED: _____ TIME: _____

PORT ARRIVED: _____ TIME: _____

SKIPPER: _____ CREW: _____

_____

GUESTS ABOARD: _____

_____

WEATHER: _____

WHAT & WHERE WE ATE: _____

_____

_____

_____

_____

WHERE WE SHOPPED & WHAT WE BOUGHT: _____

_____

_____

_____

WHO WE MET: _____

_____

_____

_____

Memorable Things About Today's Cruise

_____

_____

_____

_____

_____

_____

_____

_____

_____

REMINDER FOR NEXT PORT: _____

Today's Cruise

DAY, DATE: _____

PLANNED DESTINATION: _____

PORT DEPARTED: _____ TIME: _____

PORT ARRIVED: _____ TIME: _____

SKIPPER: _____ CREW: _____

GUESTS ABOARD: _____

WEATHER: _____

WHAT & WHERE WE ATE: _____

_____

_____

_____

_____

WHERE WE SHOPPED & WHAT WE BOUGHT: _____

_____

_____

_____

WHO WE MET: _____

_____

_____

_____

Memorable Things About Today's Cruise

_____

_____

_____

_____

_____

_____

_____

_____

PAGE_____

REMINDER FOR NEXT PORT: _____

Today's Cruise

DAY, DATE: _____

PLANNED DESTINATION: _____

PORT DEPARTED: _____ TIME: _____

PORT ARRIVED: _____ TIME: _____

SKIPPER: _____ CREW: _____

_____

GUESTS ABOARD: _____

_____

WEATHER: _____

WHAT & WHERE WE ATE: _____

_____

_____

_____

_____

WHERE WE SHOPPED & WHAT WE BOUGHT: _____

_____

_____

_____

WHO WE MET: _____

_____

_____

_____

_____

Memorable Things About Today's Cruise

_____

_____

_____

_____

_____

_____

_____

_____

_____

REMINDER FOR NEXT PORT: _____

Today's Cruise

DAY, DATE: _____

PLANNED DESTINATION: _____

PORT DEPARTED: _____ TIME: _____

PORT ARRIVED: _____ TIME: _____

SKIPPER: _____ CREW: _____

_____

GUESTS ABOARD: _____

_____

WEATHER: _____

WHAT & WHERE WE ATE: _____

_____

_____

_____

_____

_____

WHERE WE SHOPPED & WHAT WE BOUGHT: _____

_____

_____

_____

_____

WHO WE MET: _____

_____

_____

_____

_____

Memorable Things About Today's Cruise

_____

_____

_____

_____

_____

_____

_____

_____

_____

REMINDER FOR NEXT PORT: _____

Today's Cruise

DAY, DATE: _____

PLANNED DESTINATION: _____

PORT DEPARTED: _____ TIME: _____

PORT ARRIVED: _____ TIME: _____

SKIPPER: _____ CREW: _____

_____

GUESTS ABOARD: _____

_____

WEATHER: _____

WHAT & WHERE WE ATE: _____

_____

_____

_____

_____

WHERE WE SHOPPED & WHAT WE BOUGHT: _____

_____

_____

_____

_____

WHO WE MET: _____

_____

_____

_____

_____

Memorable Things About Today's Cruise

_____

_____

_____

_____

_____

_____

_____

_____

_____

REMINDER FOR NEXT PORT: _____

Today's Cruise

DAY, DATE: _____

PLANNED DESTINATION: _____

PORT DEPARTED: _____ TIME: _____

PORT ARRIVED: _____ TIME: _____

SKIPPER: _____ CREW: _____

_____

GUESTS ABOARD: _____

_____

WEATHER: _____

WHAT & WHERE WE ATE: _____

_____

_____

_____

_____

WHERE WE SHOPPED & WHAT WE BOUGHT: _____

_____

_____

_____

_____

WHO WE MET: _____

_____

_____

_____

_____

Memorable Things About Today's Cruise

_____

_____

_____

_____

_____

_____

_____

_____

_____

REMINDER FOR NEXT PORT: _____

Today's Cruise

DAY, DATE: _____

PLANNED DESTINATION: _____

PORT DEPARTED: _____ TIME: _____

PORT ARRIVED: _____ TIME: _____

SKIPPER: _____ CREW: _____

_____

GUESTS ABOARD: _____

_____

WEATHER: _____

WHAT & WHERE WE ATE: _____

_____

_____

_____

_____

WHERE WE SHOPPED & WHAT WE BOUGHT: _____

_____

_____

_____

_____

WHO WE MET: _____

_____

_____

_____

_____

Memorable Things About Today's Cruise

_____

_____

_____

_____

_____

_____

_____

_____

_____

REMINDER FOR NEXT PORT: _____

Today's Cruise

DAY, DATE: _____

PLANNED DESTINATION: _____

PORT DEPARTED: _____ TIME: _____

PORT ARRIVED: _____ TIME: _____

SKIPPER: _____ CREW: _____

_____

GUESTS ABOARD: _____

_____

WEATHER: _____

WHAT & WHERE WE ATE: _____

_____

_____

_____

_____

WHERE WE SHOPPED & WHAT WE BOUGHT: _____

_____

_____

_____

WHO WE MET: _____

_____

_____

_____

Memorable Things About Today's Cruise

_____

_____

_____

_____

_____

_____

_____

_____

REMINDER FOR NEXT PORT: _____

Today's Cruise

DAY, DATE: _____

PLANNED DESTINATION: _____

PORT DEPARTED: _____ TIME: _____

PORT ARRIVED: _____ TIME: _____

SKIPPER: _____ CREW: _____

_____

GUESTS ABOARD: _____

_____

WEATHER: _____

WHAT & WHERE WE ATE: _____

_____

_____

_____

_____

_____

WHERE WE SHOPPED & WHAT WE BOUGHT: _____

_____

_____

_____

WHO WE MET: _____

_____

_____

_____

Memorable Things About Today's Cruise

_____

_____

_____

_____

_____

_____

_____

_____

REMINDER FOR NEXT PORT: _____

Today's Cruise

DAY, DATE: _____

PLANNED DESTINATION: _____

PORT DEPARTED: _____ TIME: _____

PORT ARRIVED: _____ TIME: _____

SKIPPER: _____ CREW: _____

_____

GUESTS ABOARD: _____

_____

WEATHER: _____

WHAT & WHERE WE ATE: _____

_____

_____

_____

_____

WHERE WE SHOPPED & WHAT WE BOUGHT: _____

_____

_____

_____

WHO WE MET: _____

_____

_____

_____

Memorable Things About Today's Cruise

_____

_____

_____

_____

_____

_____

_____

_____

REMINDER FOR NEXT PORT: _____

Today's Cruise

DAY, DATE: _____

PLANNED DESTINATION: _____

PORT DEPARTED: _____ TIME: _____

PORT ARRIVED: _____ TIME: _____

SKIPPER: _____ CREW: _____

_____

GUESTS ABOARD: _____

_____

WEATHER: _____

WHAT & WHERE WE ATE: _____

_____

_____

_____

_____

WHERE WE SHOPPED & WHAT WE BOUGHT: _____

_____

_____

_____

_____

WHO WE MET: _____

_____

_____

_____

Memorable Things About Today's Cruise

_____

_____

_____

_____

_____

_____

_____

_____

REMINDER FOR NEXT PORT: _____

Today's Cruise

DAY, DATE: _____

PLANNED DESTINATION: _____

PORT DEPARTED: _____ TIME: _____

PORT ARRIVED: _____ TIME: _____

SKIPPER: _____ CREW: _____
_____

GUESTS ABOARD: _____
_____

WEATHER: _____

WHAT & WHERE WE ATE: _____
_____
_____
_____
_____

WHERE WE SHOPPED & WHAT WE BOUGHT: _____
_____
_____
_____

WHO WE MET: _____
_____
_____
_____

Memorable Things About Today's Cruise

_____
_____
_____
_____
_____
_____
_____
_____
_____

REMINDER FOR NEXT PORT: _____

Today's Cruise

DAY, DATE: _____

PLANNED DESTINATION: _____

PORT DEPARTED: _____ TIME: _____

PORT ARRIVED: _____ TIME: _____

SKIPPER: _____ CREW: _____

_____

GUESTS ABOARD: _____

_____

WEATHER: _____

WHAT & WHERE WE ATE: _____

_____

_____

_____

_____

WHERE WE SHOPPED & WHAT WE BOUGHT: _____

_____

_____

_____

WHO WE MET: _____

_____

_____

_____

_____

Memorable Things About Today's Cruise

_____

_____

_____

_____

_____

_____

_____

_____

_____

REMINDER FOR NEXT PORT: _____

Today's Cruise

DAY, DATE: _____

PLANNED DESTINATION: _____

PORT DEPARTED: _____ TIME: _____

PORT ARRIVED: _____ TIME: _____

SKIPPER: _____ CREW: _____

_____

GUESTS ABOARD: _____

_____

WEATHER: _____

WHAT & WHERE WE ATE: _____

_____

_____

_____

_____

WHERE WE SHOPPED & WHAT WE BOUGHT: _____

_____

_____

_____

WHO WE MET: _____

_____

_____

_____

_____

Memorable Things About Today's Cruise

_____

_____

_____

_____

_____

_____

_____

_____

_____

REMINDER FOR NEXT PORT: _____

Today's Cruise

DAY, DATE: _____

PLANNED DESTINATION: _____

PORT DEPARTED: _____ TIME: _____

PORT ARRIVED: _____ TIME: _____

SKIPPER: _____ CREW: _____

_____

GUESTS ABOARD: _____

_____

WEATHER: _____

WHAT & WHERE WE ATE: _____

_____

_____

_____

_____

_____

WHERE WE SHOPPED & WHAT WE BOUGHT: _____

_____

_____

_____

_____

WHO WE MET: _____

_____

_____

_____

_____

Memorable Things About Today's Cruise

_____

_____

_____

_____

_____

_____

_____

_____

_____

_____

REMINDER FOR NEXT PORT: _____

Today's Cruise

DAY, DATE: _____

PLANNED DESTINATION: _____

PORT DEPARTED: _____ TIME: _____

PORT ARRIVED: _____ TIME: _____

SKIPPER: _____ CREW: _____

_____

GUESTS ABOARD: _____

_____

WEATHER: _____

WHAT & WHERE WE ATE: _____

_____

_____

_____

_____

_____

WHERE WE SHOPPED & WHAT WE BOUGHT: _____

_____

_____

_____

WHO WE MET: _____

_____

_____

_____

_____

Memorable Things About Today's Cruise

_____

_____

_____

_____

_____

_____

_____

_____

_____

REMINDER FOR NEXT PORT: _____

Today's Cruise

DAY, DATE: _____

PLANNED DESTINATION: _____

PORT DEPARTED: _____ TIME: _____

PORT ARRIVED: _____ TIME: _____

SKIPPER: _____ CREW: _____

_____

GUESTS ABOARD: _____

_____

WEATHER: _____

WHAT & WHERE WE ATE: _____

_____

_____

_____

_____

WHERE WE SHOPPED & WHAT WE BOUGHT: _____

_____

_____

_____

WHO WE MET: _____

_____

_____

_____

Memorable Things About Today's Cruise

_____

_____

_____

_____

_____

_____

_____

_____

REMINDER FOR NEXT PORT: _____

Today's Cruise

DAY, DATE: _____

PLANNED DESTINATION: _____

PORT DEPARTED: _____ TIME: _____

PORT ARRIVED: _____ TIME: _____

SKIPPER: _____ CREW: _____

_____

GUESTS ABOARD: _____

_____

WEATHER: _____

WHAT & WHERE WE ATE: _____

_____

_____

_____

_____

WHERE WE SHOPPED & WHAT WE BOUGHT: _____

_____

_____

_____

_____

WHO WE MET: _____

_____

_____

_____

Memorable Things About Today's Cruise

_____

_____

_____

_____

_____

_____

_____

_____

_____

REMINDER FOR NEXT PORT: _____

Today's Cruise

DAY, DATE: _____

PLANNED DESTINATION: _____

PORT DEPARTED: _____ TIME: _____

PORT ARRIVED: _____ TIME: _____

SKIPPER: _____ CREW: _____

_____

GUESTS ABOARD: _____

_____

WEATHER: _____

WHAT & WHERE WE ATE: _____

_____

_____

_____

_____

WHERE WE SHOPPED & WHAT WE BOUGHT: _____

_____

_____

_____

WHO WE MET: _____

_____

_____

_____

Memorable Things About Today's Cruise

_____

_____

_____

_____

_____

_____

_____

_____

REMINDER FOR NEXT PORT: _____

Today's Cruise

DAY, DATE: _____

PLANNED DESTINATION: _____

PORT DEPARTED: _____ TIME: _____

PORT ARRIVED: _____ TIME: _____

SKIPPER: _____ CREW: _____

_____

GUESTS ABOARD: _____

_____

WEATHER: _____

WHAT & WHERE WE ATE: _____

_____

_____

_____

_____

WHERE WE SHOPPED & WHAT WE BOUGHT: _____

_____

_____

_____

WHO WE MET: _____

_____

_____

_____

Memorable Things About Today's Cruise

_____

_____

_____

_____

_____

_____

_____

_____

REMINDER FOR NEXT PORT: _____

Today's Cruise

DAY, DATE: _____

PLANNED DESTINATION: _____

PORT DEPARTED: _____ TIME: _____

PORT ARRIVED: _____ TIME: _____

SKIPPER: _____ CREW: _____

_____

GUESTS ABOARD: _____

_____

WEATHER: _____

WHAT & WHERE WE ATE: _____

_____

_____

_____

_____

WHERE WE SHOPPED & WHAT WE BOUGHT: _____

_____

_____

_____

WHO WE MET: _____

_____

_____

_____

Memorable Things About Today's Cruise

_____

_____

_____

_____

_____

_____

_____

_____

_____

REMINDER FOR NEXT PORT: _____

Today's Cruise

DAY, DATE: _____

PLANNED DESTINATION: _____

PORT DEPARTED: _____ TIME: _____

PORT ARRIVED: _____ TIME: _____

SKIPPER: _____ CREW: _____

_____

GUESTS ABOARD: _____

_____

WEATHER: _____

WHAT & WHERE WE ATE: _____

_____

_____

_____

_____

WHERE WE SHOPPED & WHAT WE BOUGHT: _____

_____

_____

_____

WHO WE MET: _____

_____

_____

_____

_____

Memorable Things About Today's Cruise

_____

_____

_____

_____

_____

_____

_____

_____

_____

REMINDER FOR NEXT PORT: _____

Today's Cruise

DAY, DATE: _____

PLANNED DESTINATION: _____

PORT DEPARTED: _____ TIME: _____

PORT ARRIVED: _____ TIME: _____

SKIPPER: _____ CREW: _____

_____

GUESTS ABOARD: _____

_____

WEATHER: _____

WHAT & WHERE WE ATE: _____

_____

_____

_____

_____

WHERE WE SHOPPED & WHAT WE BOUGHT: _____

_____

_____

_____

_____

WHO WE MET: _____

_____

_____

_____

_____

Memorable Things About Today's Cruise

_____

_____

_____

_____

_____

_____

_____

_____

_____

REMINDER FOR NEXT PORT: _____

Today's Cruise

DAY, DATE: _____

PLANNED DESTINATION: _____

PORT DEPARTED: _____ TIME: _____

PORT ARRIVED: _____ TIME: _____

SKIPPER: _____ CREW: _____

_____

GUESTS ABOARD: _____

_____

WEATHER: _____

WHAT & WHERE WE ATE: _____

_____

_____

_____

_____

WHERE WE SHOPPED & WHAT WE BOUGHT: _____

_____

_____

_____

_____

WHO WE MET: _____

_____

_____

_____

_____

Memorable Things About Today's Cruise

_____

_____

_____

_____

_____

_____

_____

_____

_____

REMINDER FOR NEXT PORT: _____

Today's Cruise

DAY, DATE: _____

PLANNED DESTINATION: _____

PORT DEPARTED: _____ TIME: _____

PORT ARRIVED: _____ TIME: _____

SKIPPER: _____ CREW: _____

_____

GUESTS ABOARD: _____

_____

WEATHER: _____

WHAT & WHERE WE ATE: _____

_____

_____

_____

_____

WHERE WE SHOPPED & WHAT WE BOUGHT: _____

_____

_____

_____

_____

WHO WE MET: _____

_____

_____

_____

_____

Memorable Things About Today's Cruise

_____

_____

_____

_____

_____

_____

_____

_____

_____

_____

REMINDER FOR NEXT PORT: _____

Today's Cruise

DAY, DATE: _____

PLANNED DESTINATION: _____

PORT DEPARTED: _____ TIME: _____

PORT ARRIVED: _____ TIME: _____

SKIPPER: _____ CREW: _____

_____

GUESTS ABOARD: _____

_____

WEATHER: _____

WHAT & WHERE WE ATE: _____

_____

_____

_____

_____

WHERE WE SHOPPED & WHAT WE BOUGHT: _____

_____

_____

_____

WHO WE MET: _____

_____

_____

_____

Memorable Things About Today's Cruise

_____

_____

_____

_____

_____

_____

_____

_____

_____

REMINDER FOR NEXT PORT: _____

Today's Cruise

DAY, DATE: _____

PLANNED DESTINATION: _____

PORT DEPARTED: _____ TIME: _____

PORT ARRIVED: _____ TIME: _____

SKIPPER: _____ CREW: _____

_____

GUESTS ABOARD: _____

_____

WEATHER: _____

WHAT & WHERE WE ATE: _____

_____

_____

_____

_____

WHERE WE SHOPPED & WHAT WE BOUGHT: _____

_____

_____

_____

_____

WHO WE MET: _____

_____

_____

_____

_____

Memorable Things About Today's Cruise

_____

_____

_____

_____

_____

_____

_____

_____

REMINDER FOR NEXT PORT: _____

Today's Cruise

DAY, DATE: _____

PLANNED DESTINATION: _____

PORT DEPARTED: _____ TIME: _____

PORT ARRIVED: _____ TIME: _____

SKIPPER: _____ CREW: _____

_____

GUESTS ABOARD: _____

_____

WEATHER: _____

WHAT & WHERE WE ATE: _____

_____

_____

_____

_____

WHERE WE SHOPPED & WHAT WE BOUGHT: _____

_____

_____

_____

WHO WE MET: _____

_____

_____

_____

Memorable Things About Today's Cruise

_____

_____

_____

_____

_____

_____

_____

_____

_____

REMINDER FOR NEXT PORT: _____

Today's Cruise

DAY, DATE: _____

PLANNED DESTINATION: _____

PORT DEPARTED: _____ TIME: _____

PORT ARRIVED: _____ TIME: _____

SKIPPER: _____ CREW: _____

_____

GUESTS ABOARD: _____

_____

WEATHER: _____

WHAT & WHERE WE ATE: _____

_____

_____

_____

_____

WHERE WE SHOPPED & WHAT WE BOUGHT: _____

_____

_____

_____

WHO WE MET: _____

_____

_____

_____

Memorable Things About Today's Cruise

_____

_____

_____

_____

_____

_____

_____

_____

_____

REMINDER FOR NEXT PORT: _____

Today's Cruise

DAY, DATE: _____

PLANNED DESTINATION: _____

PORT DEPARTED: _____ TIME: _____

PORT ARRIVED: _____ TIME: _____

SKIPPER: _____ CREW: _____

_____

GUESTS ABOARD: _____

_____

WEATHER: _____

WHAT & WHERE WE ATE: _____

_____

_____

_____

_____

WHERE WE SHOPPED & WHAT WE BOUGHT: _____

_____

_____

_____

WHO WE MET: _____

_____

_____

_____

Memorable Things About Today's Cruise

_____

_____

_____

_____

_____

_____

_____

_____

REMINDER FOR NEXT PORT: _____

Today's Cruise

DAY, DATE: _____

PLANNED DESTINATION: _____

PORT DEPARTED: _____ TIME: _____

PORT ARRIVED: _____ TIME: _____

SKIPPER: _____ CREW: _____

_____

GUESTS ABOARD: _____

_____

WEATHER: _____

WHAT & WHERE WE ATE: _____

_____

_____

_____

_____

WHERE WE SHOPPED & WHAT WE BOUGHT: _____

_____

_____

_____

_____

WHO WE MET: _____

_____

_____

_____

_____

Memorable Things About Today's Cruise

_____

_____

_____

_____

_____

_____

_____

_____

_____

REMINDER FOR NEXT PORT: _____

Today's Cruise

DAY, DATE: _____

PLANNED DESTINATION: _____

PORT DEPARTED: _____ TIME: _____

PORT ARRIVED: _____ TIME: _____

SKIPPER: _____ CREW: _____

_____

GUESTS ABOARD: _____

_____

WEATHER: _____

WHAT & WHERE WE ATE: _____

_____

_____

_____

_____

WHERE WE SHOPPED & WHAT WE BOUGHT: _____

_____

_____

_____

_____

WHO WE MET: _____

_____

_____

_____

_____

Memorable Things About Today's Cruise

_____

_____

_____

_____

_____

_____

_____

_____

_____

REMINDER FOR NEXT PORT: _____

Today's Cruise

DAY, DATE: _____

PLANNED DESTINATION: _____

PORT DEPARTED: _____ TIME: _____

PORT ARRIVED: _____ TIME: _____

SKIPPER: _____ CREW: _____

_____

GUESTS ABOARD: _____

_____

WEATHER: _____

WHAT & WHERE WE ATE: _____

_____

_____

_____

_____

WHERE WE SHOPPED & WHAT WE BOUGHT: _____

_____

_____

_____

WHO WE MET: _____

_____

_____

_____

Memorable Things About Today's Cruise

_____

_____

_____

_____

_____

_____

_____

_____

_____

REMINDER FOR NEXT PORT: _____

Today's Cruise

DAY, DATE: _____

PLANNED DESTINATION: _____

PORT DEPARTED: _____ TIME: _____

PORT ARRIVED: _____ TIME: _____

SKIPPER: _____ CREW: _____

_____

GUESTS ABOARD: _____

_____

WEATHER: _____

WHAT & WHERE WE ATE: _____

_____

_____

_____

_____

WHERE WE SHOPPED & WHAT WE BOUGHT: _____

_____

_____

_____

_____

WHO WE MET: _____

_____

_____

_____

Memorable Things About Today's Cruise

_____

_____

_____

_____

_____

_____

_____

_____

_____

REMINDER FOR NEXT PORT: _____

Today's Cruise

DAY, DATE: _____

PLANNED DESTINATION: _____

PORT DEPARTED: _____ TIME: _____

PORT ARRIVED: _____ TIME: _____

SKIPPER: _____ CREW: _____

_____

GUESTS ABOARD: _____

_____

WEATHER: _____

WHAT & WHERE WE ATE: _____

_____

_____

_____

_____

WHERE WE SHOPPED & WHAT WE BOUGHT: _____

_____

_____

_____

_____

WHO WE MET: _____

_____

_____

_____

Memorable Things About Today's Cruise

_____

_____

_____

_____

_____

_____

_____

_____

REMINDER FOR NEXT PORT: _____

Today's Cruise

DAY, DATE: _____

PLANNED DESTINATION: _____

PORT DEPARTED: _____ TIME: _____

PORT ARRIVED: _____ TIME: _____

SKIPPER: _____ CREW: _____

_____

GUESTS ABOARD: _____

_____

WEATHER: _____

WHAT & WHERE WE ATE: _____

_____

_____

_____

_____

WHERE WE SHOPPED & WHAT WE BOUGHT: _____

_____

_____

_____

_____

WHO WE MET: _____

_____

_____

_____

_____

Memorable Things About Today's Cruise

_____

_____

_____

_____

_____

_____

_____

_____

_____

REMINDER FOR NEXT PORT: _____

Today's Cruise

DAY, DATE: _____

PLANNED DESTINATION: _____

PORT DEPARTED: _____ TIME: _____

PORT ARRIVED: _____ TIME: _____

SKIPPER: _____ CREW: _____

_____

GUESTS ABOARD: _____

_____

WEATHER: _____

WHAT & WHERE WE ATE: _____

_____

_____

_____

_____

WHERE WE SHOPPED & WHAT WE BOUGHT: _____

_____

_____

_____

WHO WE MET: _____

_____

_____

_____

Memorable Things About Today's Cruise

_____

_____

_____

_____

_____

_____

_____

_____

REMINDER FOR NEXT PORT: _____

Today's Cruise

DAY, DATE: _____

PLANNED DESTINATION: _____

PORT DEPARTED: _____ TIME: _____

PORT ARRIVED: _____ TIME: _____

SKIPPER: _____ CREW: _____

_____

GUESTS ABOARD: _____

_____

WEATHER: _____

WHAT & WHERE WE ATE: _____

_____

_____

_____

_____

WHERE WE SHOPPED & WHAT WE BOUGHT: _____

_____

_____

_____

_____

WHO WE MET: _____

_____

_____

_____

_____

Memorable Things About Today's Cruise

_____

_____

_____

_____

_____

_____

_____

_____

_____

REMINDER FOR NEXT PORT: _____

Today's Cruise

DAY, DATE: _____

PLANNED DESTINATION: _____

PORT DEPARTED: _____ TIME: _____

PORT ARRIVED: _____ TIME: _____

SKIPPER: _____ CREW: _____

_____

GUESTS ABOARD: _____

_____

WEATHER: _____

WHAT & WHERE WE ATE: _____

_____

_____

_____

_____

WHERE WE SHOPPED & WHAT WE BOUGHT: _____

_____

_____

_____

WHO WE MET: _____

_____

_____

_____

_____

Memorable Things About Today's Cruise

_____

_____

_____

_____

_____

_____

_____

_____

_____

REMINDER FOR NEXT PORT: _____

Today's Cruise

DAY, DATE: _____

PLANNED DESTINATION: _____

PORT DEPARTED: _____ TIME: _____

PORT ARRIVED: _____ TIME: _____

SKIPPER: _____ CREW: _____

_____

GUESTS ABOARD: _____

_____

WEATHER: _____

WHAT & WHERE WE ATE: _____

_____

_____

_____

_____

WHERE WE SHOPPED & WHAT WE BOUGHT: _____

_____

_____

_____

_____

WHO WE MET: _____

_____

_____

_____

_____

Memorable Things About Today's Cruise

_____

_____

_____

_____

_____

_____

_____

_____

_____

REMINDER FOR NEXT PORT: _____

Today's Cruise

DAY, DATE: _____

PLANNED DESTINATION: _____

PORT DEPARTED: _____ TIME: _____

PORT ARRIVED: _____ TIME: _____

SKIPPER: _____ CREW: _____

_____

GUESTS ABOARD: _____

_____

WEATHER: _____

WHAT & WHERE WE ATE: _____

_____

_____

_____

_____

WHERE WE SHOPPED & WHAT WE BOUGHT: _____

_____

_____

_____

WHO WE MET: _____

_____

_____

_____

Memorable Things About Today's Cruise

_____

_____

_____

_____

_____

_____

_____

_____

REMINDER FOR NEXT PORT: _____

Today's Cruise

DAY, DATE: _____

PLANNED DESTINATION: _____

PORT DEPARTED: _____ TIME: _____

PORT ARRIVED: _____ TIME: _____

SKIPPER: _____ CREW: _____

_____

GUESTS ABOARD: _____

_____

WEATHER: _____

WHAT & WHERE WE ATE: _____

_____

_____

_____

_____

WHERE WE SHOPPED & WHAT WE BOUGHT: _____

_____

_____

_____

WHO WE MET: _____

_____

_____

_____

Memorable Things About Today's Cruise

_____

_____

_____

_____

_____

_____

_____

_____

_____

REMINDER FOR NEXT PORT: _____

Today's Cruise

DAY, DATE: _____

PLANNED DESTINATION: _____

PORT DEPARTED: _____ TIME: _____

PORT ARRIVED: _____ TIME: _____

SKIPPER: _____ CREW: _____

_____

GUESTS ABOARD: _____

_____

WEATHER: _____

WHAT & WHERE WE ATE: _____

_____

_____

_____

_____

WHERE WE SHOPPED & WHAT WE BOUGHT: _____

_____

_____

_____

_____

WHO WE MET: _____

_____

_____

_____

_____

Memorable Things About Today's Cruise

_____

_____

_____

_____

_____

_____

_____

_____

_____

REMINDER FOR NEXT PORT: _____

Today's Cruise

DAY, DATE: _____

PLANNED DESTINATION: _____

PORT DEPARTED: _____ TIME: _____

PORT ARRIVED: _____ TIME: _____

SKIPPER: _____ CREW: _____

_____

GUESTS ABOARD: _____

_____

WEATHER: _____

WHAT & WHERE WE ATE: _____

_____

_____

_____

_____

WHERE WE SHOPPED & WHAT WE BOUGHT: _____

_____

_____

_____

WHO WE MET: _____

_____

_____

_____

Memorable Things About Today's Cruise

_____

_____

_____

_____

_____

_____

_____

_____

REMINDER FOR NEXT PORT: _____

Today's Cruise

DAY, DATE: _____

PLANNED DESTINATION: _____

PORT DEPARTED: _____ TIME: _____

PORT ARRIVED: _____ TIME: _____

SKIPPER: _____ CREW: _____

_____

GUESTS ABOARD: _____

_____

WEATHER: _____

WHAT & WHERE WE ATE: _____

_____

_____

_____

_____

WHERE WE SHOPPED & WHAT WE BOUGHT: _____

_____

_____

_____

WHO WE MET: _____

_____

_____

_____

Memorable Things About Today's Cruise

_____

_____

_____

_____

_____

_____

_____

_____

REMINDER FOR NEXT PORT: _____

Today's Cruise

DAY, DATE: _____

PLANNED DESTINATION: _____

PORT DEPARTED: _____ TIME: _____

PORT ARRIVED: _____ TIME: _____

SKIPPER: _____ CREW: _____

_____

GUESTS ABOARD: _____

_____

WEATHER: _____

WHAT & WHERE WE ATE: _____

_____

_____

_____

_____

WHERE WE SHOPPED & WHAT WE BOUGHT: _____

_____

_____

_____

WHO WE MET: _____

_____

_____

_____

Memorable Things About Today's Cruise

_____

_____

_____

_____

_____

_____

_____

_____

_____

REMINDER FOR NEXT PORT: _____

Today's Cruise

DAY, DATE: _____

PLANNED DESTINATION: _____

PORT DEPARTED: _____ TIME: _____

PORT ARRIVED: _____ TIME: _____

SKIPPER: _____ CREW: _____

_____

GUESTS ABOARD: _____

_____

WEATHER: _____

WHAT & WHERE WE ATE: _____

_____

_____

_____

_____

WHERE WE SHOPPED & WHAT WE BOUGHT: _____

_____

_____

_____

WHO WE MET: _____

_____

_____

_____

Memorable Things About Today's Cruise

_____

_____

_____

_____

_____

_____

_____

_____

REMINDER FOR NEXT PORT: _____

Today's Cruise

DAY, DATE: _____

PLANNED DESTINATION: _____

PORT DEPARTED: _____ TIME: _____

PORT ARRIVED: _____ TIME: _____

SKIPPER: _____ CREW: _____

GUESTS ABOARD: _____

WEATHER: _____

WHAT & WHERE WE ATE: _____

_____

_____

_____

_____

WHERE WE SHOPPED & WHAT WE BOUGHT: _____

_____

_____

_____

WHO WE MET: _____

_____

_____

_____

Memorable Things About Today's Cruise

_____

_____

_____

_____

_____

_____

_____

_____

REMINDER FOR NEXT PORT: _____

Today's Cruise

DAY, DATE: _____

PLANNED DESTINATION: _____

PORT DEPARTED: _____ TIME: _____

PORT ARRIVED: _____ TIME: _____

SKIPPER: _____ CREW: _____

_____

GUESTS ABOARD: _____

_____

WEATHER: _____

WHAT & WHERE WE ATE: _____

_____

_____

_____

_____

WHERE WE SHOPPED & WHAT WE BOUGHT: _____

_____

_____

_____

WHO WE MET: _____

_____

_____

_____

Memorable Things About Today's Cruise

_____

_____

_____

_____

_____

_____

_____

_____

_____

REMINDER FOR NEXT PORT: _____

Today's Cruise

DAY, DATE: _____

PLANNED DESTINATION: _____

PORT DEPARTED: _____ TIME: _____

PORT ARRIVED: _____ TIME: _____

SKIPPER: _____ CREW: _____

_____

GUESTS ABOARD: _____

_____

WEATHER: _____

WHAT & WHERE WE ATE: _____

_____

_____

_____

_____

WHERE WE SHOPPED & WHAT WE BOUGHT: _____

_____

_____

_____

WHO WE MET: _____

_____

_____

_____

Memorable Things About Today's Cruise

_____

_____

_____

_____

_____

_____

_____

_____

PAGE_____

REMINDER FOR NEXT PORT: _____

Today's Cruise

DAY, DATE: _____

PLANNED DESTINATION: _____

PORT DEPARTED: _____ TIME: _____

PORT ARRIVED: _____ TIME: _____

SKIPPER: _____ CREW: _____

_____

GUESTS ABOARD: _____

_____

WEATHER: _____

WHAT & WHERE WE ATE: _____

_____

_____

_____

_____

WHERE WE SHOPPED & WHAT WE BOUGHT: _____

_____

_____

_____

WHO WE MET: _____

_____

_____

_____

Memorable Things About Today's Cruise

_____

_____

_____

_____

_____

_____

_____

_____

REMINDER FOR NEXT PORT: _____

Today's Cruise

DAY, DATE: _____

PLANNED DESTINATION: _____

PORT DEPARTED: _____ TIME: _____

PORT ARRIVED: _____ TIME: _____

SKIPPER: _____ CREW: _____

_____

GUESTS ABOARD: _____

_____

WEATHER: _____

WHAT & WHERE WE ATE: _____

_____

_____

_____

_____

WHERE WE SHOPPED & WHAT WE BOUGHT: _____

_____

_____

_____

WHO WE MET: _____

_____

_____

_____

_____

Memorable Things About Today's Cruise

_____

_____

_____

_____

_____

_____

_____

_____

_____

REMINDER FOR NEXT PORT: _____

Today's Cruise

DAY, DATE: _____

PLANNED DESTINATION: _____

PORT DEPARTED: _____ TIME: _____

PORT ARRIVED: _____ TIME: _____

SKIPPER: _____ CREW: _____

GUESTS ABOARD: _____

WEATHER: _____

WHAT & WHERE WE ATE: _____

_____

_____

_____

_____

WHERE WE SHOPPED & WHAT WE BOUGHT: _____

_____

_____

_____

WHO WE MET: _____

_____

_____

_____

Memorable Things About Today's Cruise

_____

_____

_____

_____

_____

_____

_____

_____

REMINDER FOR NEXT PORT: _____

Today's Cruise

DAY, DATE: _____

PLANNED DESTINATION: _____

PORT DEPARTED: _____ TIME: _____

PORT ARRIVED: _____ TIME: _____

SKIPPER: _____ CREW: _____

_____

GUESTS ABOARD: _____

_____

WEATHER: _____

WHAT & WHERE WE ATE: _____

_____

_____

_____

_____

WHERE WE SHOPPED & WHAT WE BOUGHT: _____

_____

_____

_____

WHO WE MET: _____

_____

_____

_____

Memorable Things About Today's Cruise

_____

_____

_____

_____

_____

_____

_____

_____

REMINDER FOR NEXT PORT: _____

Today's Cruise

DAY, DATE: _____

PLANNED DESTINATION: _____

PORT DEPARTED: _____ TIME: _____

PORT ARRIVED: _____ TIME: _____

SKIPPER: _____ CREW: _____

_____

GUESTS ABOARD: _____

_____

WEATHER: _____

WHAT & WHERE WE ATE: _____

_____

_____

_____

_____

WHERE WE SHOPPED & WHAT WE BOUGHT: _____

_____

_____

_____

WHO WE MET: _____

_____

_____

_____

Memorable Things About Today's Cruise

_____

_____

_____

_____

_____

_____

_____

_____

REMINDER FOR NEXT PORT: _____

Today's Cruise

DAY, DATE: _____

PLANNED DESTINATION: _____

PORT DEPARTED: _____ TIME: _____

PORT ARRIVED: _____ TIME: _____

SKIPPER: _____ CREW: _____

_____

GUESTS ABOARD: _____

_____

WEATHER: _____

WHAT & WHERE WE ATE: _____

_____

_____

_____

_____

WHERE WE SHOPPED & WHAT WE BOUGHT: _____

_____

_____

_____

WHO WE MET: _____

_____

_____

_____

Memorable Things About Today's Cruise

_____

_____

_____

_____

_____

_____

_____

_____

REMINDER FOR NEXT PORT: _____

Today's Cruise

DAY, DATE: _____

PLANNED DESTINATION: _____

PORT DEPARTED: _____ TIME: _____

PORT ARRIVED: _____ TIME: _____

SKIPPER: _____ CREW: _____

_____

GUESTS ABOARD: _____

_____

WEATHER: _____

WHAT & WHERE WE ATE: _____

_____

_____

_____

_____

WHERE WE SHOPPED & WHAT WE BOUGHT: _____

_____

_____

_____

WHO WE MET: _____

_____

_____

_____

Memorable Things About Today's Cruise

_____

_____

_____

_____

_____

_____

_____

_____

_____

REMINDER FOR NEXT PORT: _____

Today's Cruise

DAY, DATE: _____

PLANNED DESTINATION: _____

PORT DEPARTED: _____ TIME: _____

PORT ARRIVED: _____ TIME: _____

SKIPPER: _____ CREW: _____

_____

GUESTS ABOARD: _____

_____

WEATHER: _____

WHAT & WHERE WE ATE: _____

_____

_____

_____

_____

WHERE WE SHOPPED & WHAT WE BOUGHT: _____

_____

_____

_____

WHO WE MET: _____

_____

_____

_____

Memorable Things About Today's Cruise

_____

_____

_____

_____

_____

_____

_____

_____

REMINDER FOR NEXT PORT: _____

Today's Cruise

DAY, DATE: _____

PLANNED DESTINATION: _____

PORT DEPARTED: _____ TIME: _____

PORT ARRIVED: _____ TIME: _____

SKIPPER: _____ CREW: _____

_____

GUESTS ABOARD: _____

_____

WEATHER: _____

WHAT & WHERE WE ATE: _____

_____

_____

_____

_____

WHERE WE SHOPPED & WHAT WE BOUGHT: _____

_____

_____

_____

WHO WE MET: _____

_____

_____

_____

Memorable Things About Today's Cruise

_____

_____

_____

_____

_____

_____

_____

_____

REMINDER FOR NEXT PORT: _____

Today's Cruise

DAY, DATE: _____

PLANNED DESTINATION: _____

PORT DEPARTED: _____ TIME: _____

PORT ARRIVED: _____ TIME: _____

SKIPPER: _____ CREW: _____

_____

GUESTS ABOARD: _____

_____

WEATHER: _____

WHAT & WHERE WE ATE: _____

_____

_____

_____

_____

WHERE WE SHOPPED & WHAT WE BOUGHT: _____

_____

_____

_____

_____

WHO WE MET: _____

_____

_____

_____

_____

Memorable Things About Today's Cruise

_____

_____

_____

_____

_____

_____

_____

_____

_____

REMINDER FOR NEXT PORT: _____

Today's Cruise

DAY, DATE: _____

PLANNED DESTINATION: _____

PORT DEPARTED: _____ TIME: _____

PORT ARRIVED: _____ TIME: _____

SKIPPER: _____ CREW: _____

_____

GUESTS ABOARD: _____

_____

WEATHER: _____

WHAT & WHERE WE ATE: _____

_____

_____

_____

_____

WHERE WE SHOPPED & WHAT WE BOUGHT: _____

_____

_____

_____

WHO WE MET: _____

_____

_____

_____

Memorable Things About Today's Cruise

_____

_____

_____

_____

_____

_____

_____

_____

REMINDER FOR NEXT PORT: _____

Today's Cruise

DAY, DATE: _____

PLANNED DESTINATION: _____

PORT DEPARTED: _____ TIME: _____

PORT ARRIVED: _____ TIME: _____

SKIPPER: _____ CREW: _____

_____

GUESTS ABOARD: _____

_____

WEATHER: _____

WHAT & WHERE WE ATE: _____

_____

_____

_____

_____

WHERE WE SHOPPED & WHAT WE BOUGHT: _____

_____

_____

_____

_____

WHO WE MET: _____

_____

_____

_____

_____

Memorable Things About Today's Cruise

_____

_____

_____

_____

_____

_____

_____

_____

_____

REMINDER FOR NEXT PORT: _____

Today's Cruise

DAY, DATE: _____

PLANNED DESTINATION: _____

PORT DEPARTED: _____ TIME: _____

PORT ARRIVED: _____ TIME: _____

SKIPPER: _____ CREW: _____

_____

GUESTS ABOARD: _____

_____

WEATHER: _____

WHAT & WHERE WE ATE: _____

_____

_____

_____

_____

WHERE WE SHOPPED & WHAT WE BOUGHT: _____

_____

_____

_____

WHO WE MET: _____

_____

_____

_____

Memorable Things About Today's Cruise

_____

_____

_____

_____

_____

_____

_____

_____

REMINDER FOR NEXT PORT: _____

Today's Cruise

DAY, DATE: _____

PLANNED DESTINATION: _____

PORT DEPARTED: _____ TIME: _____

PORT ARRIVED: _____ TIME: _____

SKIPPER: _____ CREW: _____

_____

GUESTS ABOARD: _____

_____

WEATHER: _____

WHAT & WHERE WE ATE: _____

_____

_____

_____

_____

WHERE WE SHOPPED & WHAT WE BOUGHT: _____

_____

_____

_____

_____

WHO WE MET: _____

_____

_____

_____

_____

Memorable Things About Today's Cruise

_____

_____

_____

_____

_____

_____

_____

_____

_____

REMINDER FOR NEXT PORT: _____

Today's Cruise

DAY, DATE: _____

PLANNED DESTINATION: _____

PORT DEPARTED: _____ TIME: _____

PORT ARRIVED: _____ TIME: _____

SKIPPER: _____ CREW: _____

_____

GUESTS ABOARD: _____

_____

WEATHER: _____

WHAT & WHERE WE ATE: _____

_____

_____

_____

_____

WHERE WE SHOPPED & WHAT WE BOUGHT: _____

_____

_____

_____

WHO WE MET: _____

_____

_____

_____

Memorable Things About Today's Cruise

_____

_____

_____

_____

_____

_____

_____

_____

REMINDER FOR NEXT PORT: _____

Today's Cruise

DAY, DATE: _____

PLANNED DESTINATION: _____

PORT DEPARTED: _____ TIME: _____

PORT ARRIVED: _____ TIME: _____

SKIPPER: _____ CREW: _____
_____

GUESTS ABOARD: _____
_____

WEATHER: _____

WHAT & WHERE WE ATE: _____
_____
_____
_____
_____

WHERE WE SHOPPED & WHAT WE BOUGHT: _____
_____
_____
_____
_____

WHO WE MET: _____
_____
_____
_____
_____

Memorable Things About Today's Cruise

_____
_____
_____
_____
_____
_____
_____
_____
_____

REMINDER FOR NEXT PORT: _____

Today's Cruise

DAY, DATE: _____

PLANNED DESTINATION: _____

PORT DEPARTED: _____ TIME: _____

PORT ARRIVED: _____ TIME: _____

SKIPPER: _____ CREW: _____

_____

GUESTS ABOARD: _____

_____

WEATHER: _____

WHAT & WHERE WE ATE: _____

_____

_____

_____

_____

WHERE WE SHOPPED & WHAT WE BOUGHT: _____

_____

_____

_____

_____

WHO WE MET: _____

_____

_____

_____

Memorable Things About Today's Cruise

_____

_____

_____

_____

_____

_____

_____

_____

REMINDER FOR NEXT PORT: _____

Today's Cruise

DAY, DATE: _____

PLANNED DESTINATION: _____

PORT DEPARTED: _____ TIME: _____

PORT ARRIVED: _____ TIME: _____

SKIPPER: _____ CREW: _____

_____

GUESTS ABOARD: _____

_____

WEATHER: _____

WHAT & WHERE WE ATE: _____

_____

_____

_____

_____

WHERE WE SHOPPED & WHAT WE BOUGHT: _____

_____

_____

_____

WHO WE MET: _____

_____

_____

_____

Memorable Things About Today's Cruise

_____

_____

_____

_____

_____

_____

_____

_____

REMINDER FOR NEXT PORT: _____

Today's Cruise

DAY, DATE: _____

PLANNED DESTINATION: _____

PORT DEPARTED: _____ TIME: _____

PORT ARRIVED: _____ TIME: _____

SKIPPER: _____ CREW: _____

_____

GUESTS ABOARD: _____

_____

WEATHER: _____

WHAT & WHERE WE ATE: _____

_____

_____

_____

_____

WHERE WE SHOPPED & WHAT WE BOUGHT: _____

_____

_____

_____

WHO WE MET: _____

_____

_____

_____

Memorable Things About Today's Cruise

_____

_____

_____

_____

_____

_____

_____

_____

_____

REMINDER FOR NEXT PORT: _____

Today's Cruise

DAY, DATE: _____

PLANNED DESTINATION: _____

PORT DEPARTED: _____ TIME: _____

PORT ARRIVED: _____ TIME: _____

SKIPPER: _____ CREW: _____

_____

GUESTS ABOARD: _____

_____

WEATHER: _____

WHAT & WHERE WE ATE: _____

_____

_____

_____

_____

WHERE WE SHOPPED & WHAT WE BOUGHT: _____

_____

_____

_____

WHO WE MET: _____

_____

_____

_____

_____

Memorable Things About Today's Cruise

_____

_____

_____

_____

_____

_____

_____

_____

_____

_____

REMINDER FOR NEXT PORT: _____

Today's Cruise

DAY, DATE: _____

PLANNED DESTINATION: _____

PORT DEPARTED: _____ TIME: _____

PORT ARRIVED: _____ TIME: _____

SKIPPER: _____ CREW: _____

_____

GUESTS ABOARD: _____

_____

WEATHER: _____

WHAT & WHERE WE ATE: _____

_____

_____

_____

_____

WHERE WE SHOPPED & WHAT WE BOUGHT: _____

_____

_____

_____

_____

WHO WE MET: _____

_____

_____

_____

_____

Memorable Things About Today's Cruise

_____

_____

_____

_____

_____

_____

_____

_____

_____

REMINDER FOR NEXT PORT: _____

Today's Cruise

DAY, DATE: _____

PLANNED DESTINATION: _____

PORT DEPARTED: _____ TIME: _____

PORT ARRIVED: _____ TIME: _____

SKIPPER: _____ CREW: _____

_____

GUESTS ABOARD: _____

_____

WEATHER: _____

WHAT & WHERE WE ATE: _____

_____

_____

_____

_____

WHERE WE SHOPPED & WHAT WE BOUGHT: _____

_____

_____

_____

WHO WE MET: _____

_____

_____

_____

Memorable Things About Today's Cruise

_____

_____

_____

_____

_____

_____

_____

_____

REMINDER FOR NEXT PORT: _____

Today's Cruise

DAY, DATE: _____

PLANNED DESTINATION: _____

PORT DEPARTED: _____ TIME: _____

PORT ARRIVED: _____ TIME: _____

SKIPPER: _____ CREW: _____

_____

GUESTS ABOARD: _____

_____

WEATHER: _____

WHAT & WHERE WE ATE: _____

_____

_____

_____

_____

WHERE WE SHOPPED & WHAT WE BOUGHT: _____

_____

_____

_____

WHO WE MET: _____

_____

_____

_____

Memorable Things About Today's Cruise

_____

_____

_____

_____

_____

_____

_____

_____

REMINDER FOR NEXT PORT: _____

Today's Cruise

DAY, DATE: _____

PLANNED DESTINATION: _____

PORT DEPARTED: _____ TIME: _____

PORT ARRIVED: _____ TIME: _____

SKIPPER: _____ CREW: _____

_____

GUESTS ABOARD: _____

_____

WEATHER: _____

WHAT & WHERE WE ATE: _____

_____

_____

_____

_____

WHERE WE SHOPPED & WHAT WE BOUGHT: _____

_____

_____

_____

WHO WE MET: _____

_____

_____

_____

Memorable Things About Today's Cruise

_____

_____

_____

_____

_____

_____

_____

_____

_____

REMINDER FOR NEXT PORT: _____

Today's Cruise

DAY, DATE: _____

PLANNED DESTINATION: _____

PORT DEPARTED: _____ TIME: _____

PORT ARRIVED: _____ TIME: _____

SKIPPER: _____ CREW: _____

_____

GUESTS ABOARD: _____

_____

WEATHER: _____

WHAT & WHERE WE ATE: _____

_____

_____

_____

_____

WHERE WE SHOPPED & WHAT WE BOUGHT: _____

_____

_____

_____

_____

WHO WE MET: _____

_____

_____

_____

Memorable Things About Today's Cruise

_____

_____

_____

_____

_____

_____

_____

_____

_____

REMINDER FOR NEXT PORT: _____

Today's Cruise

DAY, DATE: _____

PLANNED DESTINATION: _____

PORT DEPARTED: _____ TIME: _____

PORT ARRIVED: _____ TIME: _____

SKIPPER: _____ CREW: _____

_____

GUESTS ABOARD: _____

_____

WEATHER: _____

WHAT & WHERE WE ATE: _____

_____

_____

_____

_____

WHERE WE SHOPPED & WHAT WE BOUGHT: _____

_____

_____

_____

_____

WHO WE MET: _____

_____

_____

_____

_____

Memorable Things About Today's Cruise

_____

_____

_____

_____

_____

_____

_____

_____

_____

REMINDER FOR NEXT PORT: _____

Index of Cruises

DATE	POINT OF DEPARTURE	DESTINATION	PAGE

Index of Cruises

DATE	POINT OF DEPARTURE	DESTINATION	PAGE